# EVERYTHING YOU NEED TO KNOW ABOUT THE US VOTING SYSTEM

## Government Books for Kids
## Children's Government Books

**BABY PROFESSOR**
EDUCATION KIDS

**Speedy Publishing LLC**

**40 E. Main St. #1156**

**Newark, DE 19711**

**www.speedypublishing.com**

**Copyright 2017**

**V**oting is one of the easiest, and at the same time one of the most important, tasks United States citizens have. Let's find out why it's so important and how it works.

# WHAT VOTING IS

**V**oting is stating your preference for one of two or more candidates for a position. In the United States, most of the people who make important decisions about the way the country should go are elected officials. At the top of the heap is the President of the United States, but elected officials in important jobs range all the way down from there to the members of the school board in your town.

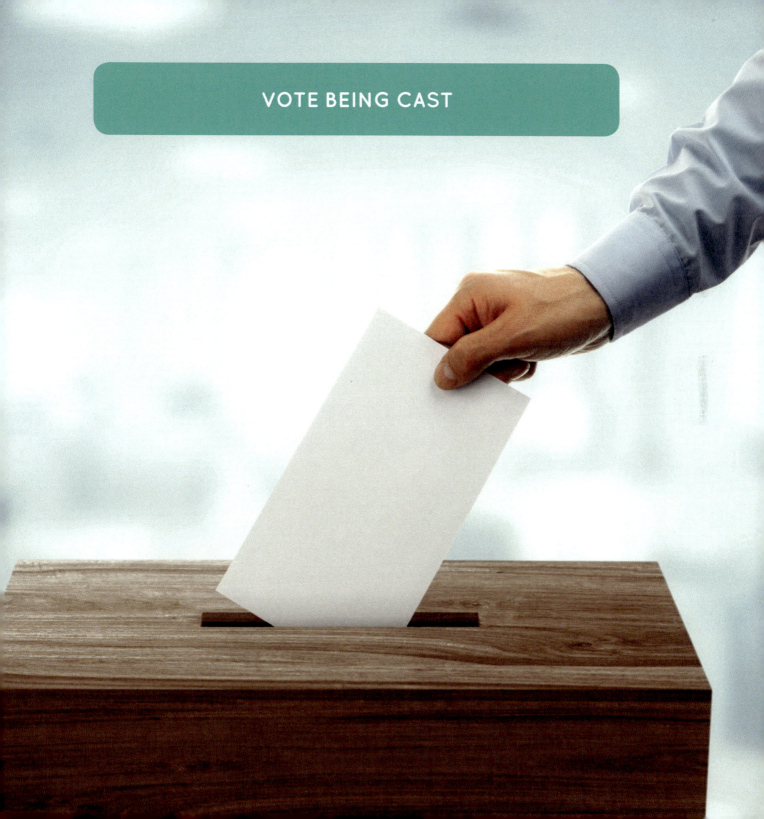

VOTE BEING CAST

**W**ho puts them in their offices? Voters do. Usually, the person who gets the most votes for a certain office gets that job for a year, two years, or even six years, so it's important to vote for the person you think will do the best job, whenever you get the chance.

# WHO WE VOTE FOR

In the U.S. we vote for candidates at three levels of government: federal, state, and local. The officials have different responsibilities and take different skills. You as a voter should try to understand what each candidate you might vote for thinks is good for the country, and how that person wants to carry out his or her job. That helps you carry out your job of voting.

AN ELECTORAL CAMPAIGN

We tend to think about just the top-level jobs, like president and vice-president, when we think of elections in the U.S. But your ballot may have dozens of races, dozens of choices you may have to make about who would best fit the job he or she wants.

# FEDERAL LEVEL

**W**e don't vote for federal judges (the "Judicial Branch"), but we do vote for:

President and Vice President. Two people run together for these jobs. When you vote, you are actually voting for people who are pledged to vote for your candidates in the "Electoral College".

MAN VOTING

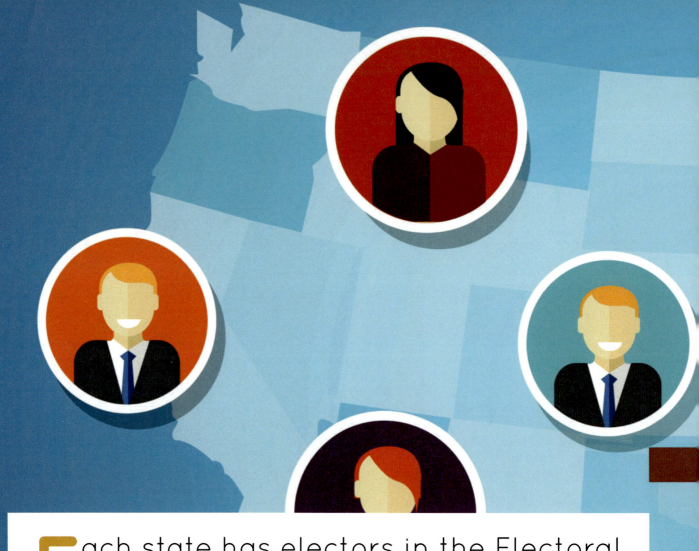

Each state has electors in the Electoral College according to its population, and the electors for each state are supposed to vote for the candidates for these two jobs who won their state. Sometimes, as in 1824,

1876, 1888, 2000, and 2016, the candidates with the smaller number of individual votes end up with the larger number of votes in the Electoral College, and become President and Vice President.

These people are the heads of the "Executive Branch" of government, responsible for getting things done. They have four-year terms, and can run for a second term of office.

The next two groups make up the "Legislative Branch" of the federal government. They write the laws and set the budgets.

ELECTION DEBATES

POLITICIANS

**Senators.** Your state has two senators, each with a six-year term. The terms are organized so usually you are only voting for one Senate seat in each election.

**Members of the House of Representatives.** Each state has at least one Representative, and the states with larger populations have a lot more. You get to vote for one of the candidates in your district within the state. Members of the House have two-year terms, so they seem to always be running for re-election!

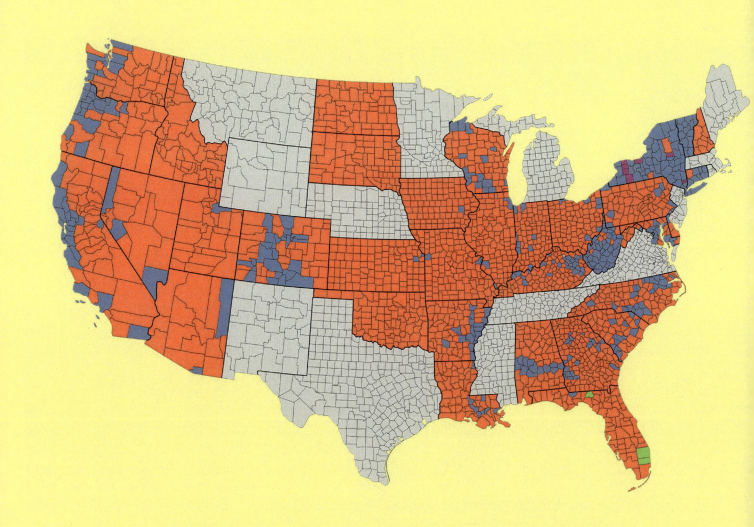

UNITED STATES ELECTION MAP

# STATE LEVEL

State government, like the federal government, has a judicial, legislative, and executive branch. Different states have different rules about terms of office, and how long anyone can be in a particular elected office.

Some states elect judges for some or all levels of the judicial branch; others don't. All states have a governor, whose term can be as little as two years or as much as four years.

You get to elect your governor and lieutenant governor, who are like the president and vice-president of your state.

THE MICHIGAN STATE CAPITOL IS THE BUILDING THAT HOUSES THE LEGISLATIVE BRANCH OF THE GOVERNMENT OF THE U.S. STATE OF MICHIGAN.

Some states have two legislative houses, like the federal House and Senate, and some have one. If your state has two, you will get to vote for whoever represents you in each house.

Some states have other jobs that you elect people to, like Commissioner of Agriculture. Check before you go to vote so you can be an informed voter!

# LOCAL LEVEL

**D**epending on your community, you may get to vote for people for these offices:

- Mayor
- City Council member
- County commissioner or other county officers
- Sheriff

CITY MAYOR

And many, many other positions, some of them with very odd titles! These positions have different terms of office in different states.

# WHO CAN VOTE

In general, you have the right to vote if you are:

- A United States citizen
- Eighteen years or older
- Registered to vote

# VOTE REGISTRATION
## APPLICATION

**Identification Information**

| | Yes | No |
|---|---|---|
| Driver license? | ☐ Yes | ☐ No |
| Leamer permit? | ☐ Yes | ☐ No |
| Non-driver ID Card? | ☐ Yes | ☐ No |

The objectives will be based on how you gain sales by acquiring and keeping customers. A marketing strategy helps on making good messages with the right twist of marketing approaches in order to have a good outcome of your sales and marketing activities.

**(Check any that apply)**

☐ **Replacement**

**Applying For A**          ☐ **Renewal**

☐ **Permit**    ☐ **ID Card**

**Your Personal**

Full Last Name          Gender  ☐ Male  ☐ Female

Full First Name

Date of birth    Day / Month / Year

Nationality

**ID card number and Details**    enter the identification number it appears on the card

Out-of-State License ID No:

**Contact Details**

Type of License:          Home Phone

Date of Expiration:          Mobil

**Your Personal Details**

Hight    cm / inches    Eye color          ☐ Devorced          **Address where**
(This address will appear

Email Address: (optional)    ☐ Married          Has your mailing address

Status:    ☐ Single                    What is the che

Others          **Other change:**  (new license e

**Address where you live**    Street

Unit No.    Street No.    Post Code

          State

Town/City

Some states make it very easy to register to vote: you may even be able to do it when you get a driver's license! Other states make it much harder to register. Also, people with criminal records in some states may have had their right to vote suspended or removed. So make sure you have done everything you need to do before election day to avoid an unhappy surprise when you go to vote!

However, at the start of the United States in 1789, each state could set the voting requirements.

Almost everywhere only white men who owned property in the state or area where the vote was being held could vote!

**L**ittle by little the right to vote (the "franchise") has been expanded. Here are some significant milestones:

- **1792:** States start abolishing the requirement to own property.
- **1870:** Non-white men and freed male slaves get the right to vote. Some states had a hard time with allowing male slaves to vote but they came around eventually.

- **1887:** Native Americans are eligible to vote.
- **1913:** Up until now, state legislatures elected the state's two senators. Starting in 1913, the general public voted directly to elect their senators.

Official Program WOMAN SUFFRAGE Procession

Votes for Women

Washington D.C. March 3, 1913

- **1920:** Women get the right to vote. As with non-white voters, some states resisted acting on this change for many years.

- **1943:** Chinese immigrants get the right to become citizens and to vote.

- **1961:** Up until now, residents of the District of Columbia could not vote for the president. In this year that changed, although Washington, D.C. is still not a state and has no senators.

- **1964:** States cannot require a "poll tax" or the payment of any fee before voting. This was a major way of depressing the number of non-white and poor voters. This applied to federal elections at first, and was extended to state elections in 1966.
- **1971:** The voting age dropped from 21 to 18.

# HOW WE VOTE

**T**he overall principle of voting in United States elections is: "by secret ballot". Nobody has the right to know how you voted, or to force you to vote for one person over another.

Election officials make every effort to make sure elections are conducted fairly, that each vote is counted properly, that nobody votes who does not have that right, and that nobody votes more than once.

ELECTION

VOTE NOW

VOTING ONLINE

Depending on the election and where you live, you might use one of these methods:

- Paper ballot that you fill in and drop into a box at a voting station.
- Electronic voting machine, also at a voting station.
- Voting by mail.
- Voting online.

- Voting by proxy: under some conditions, for some elections you can assign someone else to use your vote.
- Voting by special ballot if you are serving overseas in the military, or are living outside the country.
- Voting by secure email: if you are an astronaut on the International Space Station on election day, that's how you would vote!

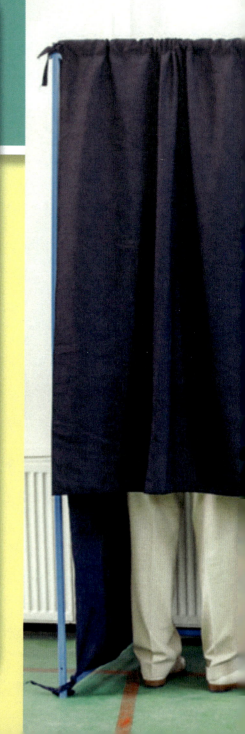

PEOPLE VOTING IN POLLING BOOTHS

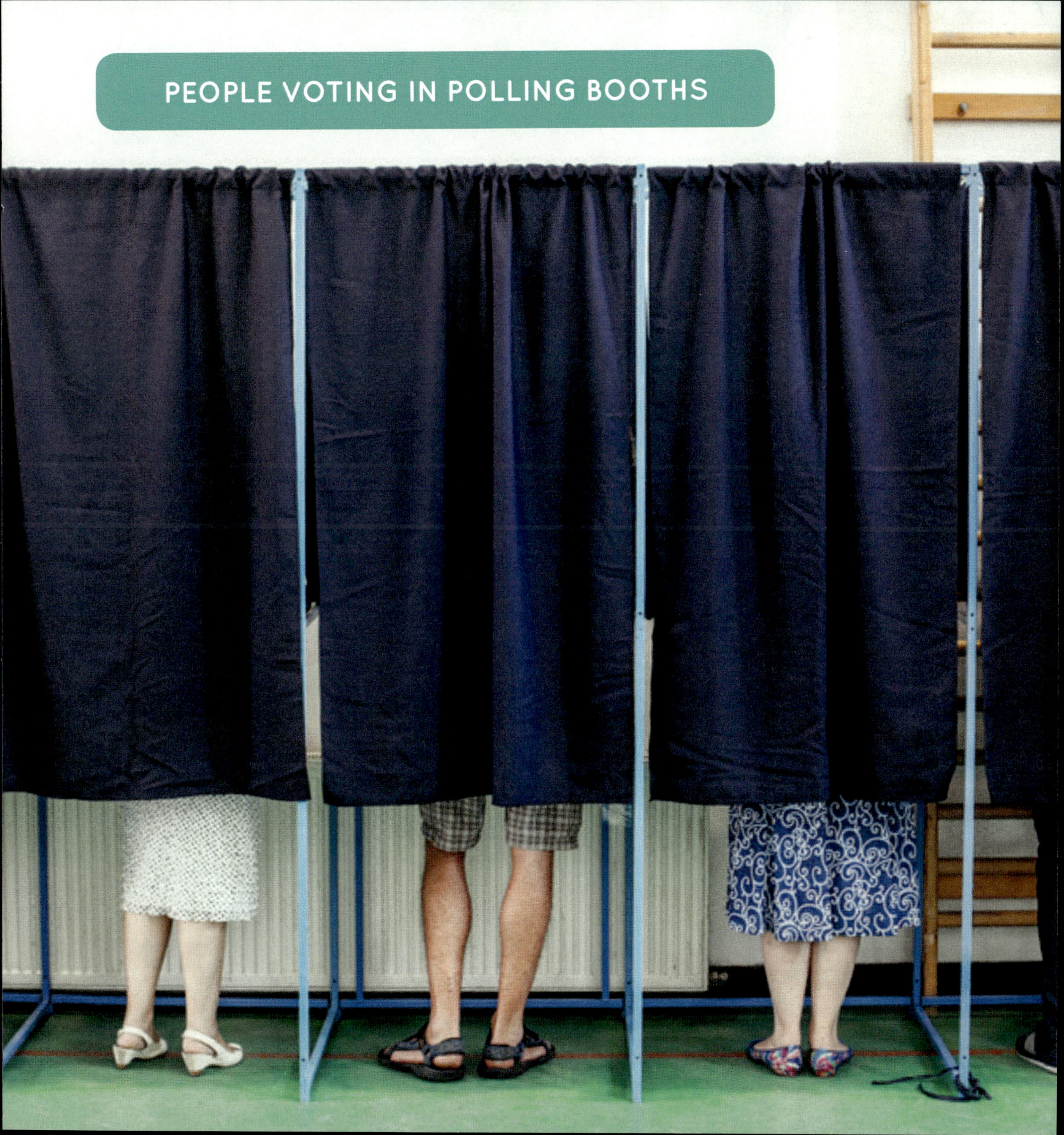

There are a lot of stories and rumors about voter fraud: people voting several times, voting under someone else's name, or in some other way running up the vote count for their candidate. In fact, the number of proven cases of voter fraud is tiny compared to all the votes cast.

A much larger issue is voter suppression, where parties or even government bodies work to make it harder for some people to vote, to prevent them voting "the wrong way". Voter suppression is a serious issue, affecting thousands of citizens, that has been ongoing since at least the time non-white people began to get the right to vote.

A new issue is electronic tampering with voting machines or the software that makes the total vote count from the input of all those machines. A real challenge here is that there are no paper ballots one can count to double-check that the machine is giving the correct answer.

HACKING THE VOTES

# WHEN WE VOTE

**F**ederal elections happen on the first Tuesday after the first Monday in November in even-numbered years. All the seats of the House of Representatives, and one third of the Senate seats, are up for election every two years. Every four years we also vote for a president and vice-president.

**A**t other levels of government, election day may be the same day as the federal election, or on another day. Check with your local officials so you don't miss it!

MAN VOTING

# A DEMOCRACY TAKES EFFORT

This may seem like a very complex process, and it is. In fact, the whole business of democratic government is complex, because it is an attempt to balance the need to get things done with the right of every citizen to contribute to the decisions of government.

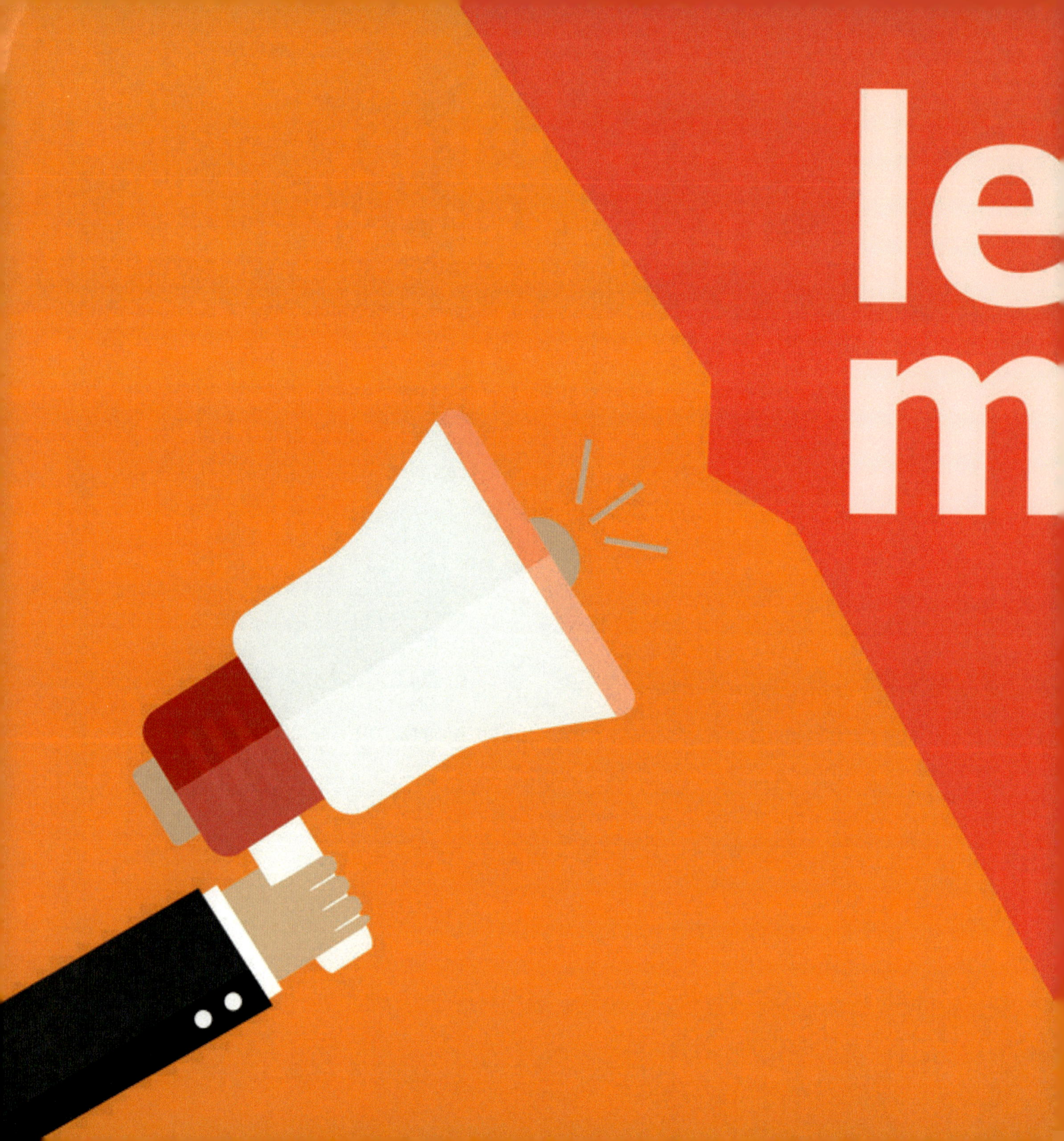
le
m

arn
ore

Learn more in the Baby Professor book
How Does the US Government Work?

Visit

**BABY PROFESSOR**
EDUCATION KIDS

# www.BabyProfessorBooks.com

to download Free Baby Professor eBooks
and view our catalog of new and exciting
Children's Books

Made in the USA
Middletown, DE
07 September 2020